Effective Habits of the Five People You Meet In Heaven

Effective Habits of the Five People You Meet In Heaven

Steve Kellmeyer

Bridegroom Press   Peoria, IL

To obtain additional copies of this book,
contact:
www.bridegroompress.com

All Scripture quotations are taken from the Douay-Rheims Bible

Copyright
July 2004
Bridegroom Press

Printed in the U.S.A.

ISBN: **0-9718128-9-6**

Cover Illustration: Yvonne Bontkowski

The journey to the mountaintop has long been associated with the journey to meet God. The cover recalls Eddie's encounter with Ruby, his third person, whom he meets in the mountains.

Contents

Introduction

Reading Mitch Albom's popular book, *The Five People You Meet in Heaven,* is a marvelously uplifting experience that allows us to reflect on the most profound of topics. In the course of this reflection, we eventually realize that all of the people he portrays share certain characteristics. We are not really surprised to discover this. We all instinctively know that certain kinds of actions and attitudes are beneficial to us, while other actions and attitudes are not. But not all of us have the ability to articulate the differences.

Because Mr. Albom has done such an excellent job in creating honest characters, it is worthwhile for us to study them and what they have to say. It is also worthwhile for us to study how Mr. Albom has accomplished his task, for he touches on the heart of a great mystery, and he does so with surpassing skill.

Like great science, great theology, or great philosophy, great art teaches deep truth. The contemplation of the beautiful necessarily brings us to a deeper understanding of the world we live in.

Through these studies we can, perhaps, come to a greater understanding of how to form our own lives into things of surpassing beauty. As we work to accomplish this, we likewise discover that we gain a measure of peace with ourselves and with each other.

Can there be any better reason to while away an hour or two? If you think as I do, then find a comfortable chair, get a mug of something to drink and let us begin.

Each of the five sections begins with a discussion of the characters and what they did in the story. This is followed by an analysis of their actions in light of their approach to the world, their habits. Each section ends with questions for discussion and other readings, as an assistance to those who would like to explore these habits more deeply.

The First Person:
The Blue Man

Ruby's Pier

Mr. Albom begins with death and so shall we. Indeed, we could hardly do better than to begin with death, for death is a fact, though little discussed. Surely few pay it close attention in this day and age. The world is busy enough, entertaining enough, to keep the fact of our deaths at a distance, at least most of the time. Some few of us are brought up short every year by a sudden illness, a grim-faced doctor, or a hurtling ton of auto-sculpted steel, but by and large, the rest of us are untouched by the fact Eddie faces at the beginning of the novel, and we are determined to remain so.

For most of us, it seems odd to think it should be any other way. True, one or two of us who enjoy reading history may recall that certain men and women slept in their coffins every night as a way of keeping their deaths constantly before them. Perhaps we remember seeing in a children's picture book a cartoon monk, dressed in drab brown, scribbling away with a feather pen at a makeshift desk, with the black sockets of a human skull wordlessly watching him work, for the medieval religious orders used to do that kind of thing. "Live life from the grave!" they cried. It seems decidedly morbid to us today, but it was not so harsh a life as one might think.

The wise men of the East have a proverb, "It is useless to threaten a man who is not afraid to die." Indeed, the whole purpose of Zen meditation and similar eastern spiritual practices is to help reconcile the student to the fact of his impending death. In this respect at least, and whatever else one might say, Eastern and Western religious traditions are agreed. The wise man prepares for what he knows he cannot avoid. Whether it be flood or famine, drought or death, the wise man prepares.

The rest of us tend to do what Eddie did at the beginning of the story. We ignore the quiet cat feet of years and debilities, in the hopes that what is silently approaching may be avoided if only we refuse to notice it is there.

Pain: Death's First Cousin

As we approach death, we often experience pain. Eddie certainly did. Pain is, of course, not something to wish on anyone. But it serves a certain purpose, if only in forcing us to face the reality of death.

Pain and death share a family resemblance. Consider. Pain is, in a sense, a poverty – it is not a "something" so much as it is a lack of something: a lack of comfort, a lack of the ability to be peaceful. Now, some go through a whole lifetime of physical pain, they live an entire life of lack, but that is rather unusual. Our bodies work painlessly for most of us, most of the time. Once we survive the illnesses of childhood, we have – for the most part – several long score of years, perhaps three-score, perhaps more, in which physical pain is an uncommon visitor. We become used to our physical affluence, the wealth of health our bodies provide us. We may be short of money, of love, of joy, but – unlike Eddie – we don't spend most of our lives with a cane in our hand or pain shooting through us at every step.

Thus, for us, the first flash of pain is something of a shock, like the sudden realization that one's wallet is missing, or one's car is not where it was left. Something has been taken. Where there was wealth, there is now a hole, a lack, an emptiness – and fear. In a heartbeat we feel the knowledge pain brings: not only is something taken but... if this can be taken, what else is at risk?

> Death is both the ultimate and the unavoidable poverty.

In that first rush of pain, the worst part is not the suffering, but the fear. What else *can* be taken? What else *is* at risk? How bad is it, doctor? A wealthy man stripped of his money finds his first weeks on the streets hard. Eating out of trashcans does not settle his stomach like the crystal glass of fine merlot had. Similarly, a healthy man finds it hard to stay in his chair or bed if only because he fears never being able to leave it. Pain is the poverty that prophecies. "This is taken now," it whispers, "but there is more yet to be taken."

The most painful part of this prophecy is its truth. We *know* more is yet to be taken. Like the buzzing alarm clock on a dreary Monday, pain awakens us to what is coming, whether we like it or not. But it does more. It not only awakens us, it begins to strip us of our self-possessions in preparation for the door we must pass through, the unspeakable: death. In this sense, the poverty of pain is good preparation, for death is both the ultimate and the unavoidable poverty.

In the movie *Unforgiven*, Clint Eastwood's character, William Munney, points out, "It's a hell of a thing to kill a man. You take everything he ever had and everything he's gonna." This is a strikingly accurate summary of the situation. In death, we not only lose every earthly possession; we even lose our molded clay bodies to the grave. All that is left is what we have made of ourselves during our lives. And that is the test.

We have heard many things about the soul over the course of our lives. Scientists dispute it, philosophers dissect it, theologians describe it, priests prepare it and charlatans sell idols to heal it. Yet we need be none of these - we need meet none of these - in order to know one thing: love is its life. If we know anything about the soul, we know this much. In the end, knowing this and living it properly is enough.

> Love is the life of the soul.

How Now Shall We Live?

But knowing a thing and living it are two different things. We can know something perfectly, but still live it badly.

Take Eddie and Dominguez for instance. They are not just maintenance men, they are fishermen. The amusement park built at "the end of the line" lies near the sea. The men fish through a small hole cut in the boards, sixty feet above the ocean. But Eddie knows what Dominguez refuses to acknowledge. Even if the fabled halibut was hooked, "you could never pull a fish that big through a hole that small."

> "You will make men as the
> fishes of the sea..."
> *Habakkuk 1:14*

Eddie may not have read Habakkuk, but he felt in his bones the connection between the uncaught halibut on the other side of that hole and himself. "How narrow is the gate and strait is the way that leads to eternal life: and few there are that find it!" (Matthew 7:14). It would be easier for a halibut to pass through the hole cut in the boards then for a man to pass body and soul through Death's narrow door. On at least some level, Eddie knows this necessary truth. Dominguez does not.

And it is Eddie alone who reasons his way to another truth. When he sees Freddy's Free Fall fail, he alone realizes the thread by which four human lives are suspended is itself on the point of breaking. The key that opens death's narrow door and allows Eddie to being his journey is the same key that snaps the cable of Freddy's Free Fall. It might be said of him "My life is cut off, as by a weaver" (Isaiah 38:12).

From Death to Life

Are you startled? By now, you may have discovered something here which you did not entirely expect. There is more to this story than meets the eye. There is indeed: much more. A great story tells its tale not only in the grand scale of the plot, but in every aspect of the tale. Every detail serves to magnify the story being told. And this is a great story.

When we speak truly of death and of what follows, we echo what has been said before. Indeed, in certain writings, the wisdom of the dead has been captured with such brilliance that we carry the suspicion the men who wrote are not truly dead. As we will see, many of the intricate details of the novel resonate within us because they echo a greater story, a Unique Story. Thus it is with all that we do. We approach greatness when we capture the essence of this one epic story in our lives and our speech, making it fresh by the breath of our words and the character of our deeds. We will discover that the details of this novel echo the One Great Story.

Consider a single example (though we will consider many more). Death begins Mr. Albom's tale, but life is its setting. We return again and again to the old amusement park, knowing that all old amusement parks are found "at the end of the line."

> "Life and death upon one tether
> and running beautifully together."
> *from "Crystal Moment"*
> *Robert Peter Tristam Coffin*

Hard by this joyful life lies that ancient symbol of discontinuity and death, the sea, surging endlessly, its pounding surf reminding us of ancient days and of "them that are slain the heart of the sea" (Ezekiel 28:8).

Much can be said about the connections between these two things, but let us begin the conversation this way. The marriage of amusement park and ocean helps us examine Eddie's approaching death without fear. Their union is natural, the two complement one another. Thus, it is perfectly natural to discover that Eddie's death, his departure from the amusement park, the end of the line and the beginning of the journey, plunges him into the sea and thereby into his new life.

Through this transition, we can see that Death is not a loss. Indeed, Death is transformed from a loss to an opportunity. What is past cannot change, but what is past affects his new life most profoundly, for this new life turns out to be a summary of all that he has been, all he strove to be.

In Greek legend, a man named Sisyphus offended the gods, and was condemned to roll a boulder to the top of a mountain. But the gods arranged it so that the boulder would always slip from his grasp before he reached the top. Thus, Sisyphus is in an eternal, useless struggle against a dead weight that will always elude his grasp in the end. He cannot win, but he is condemned to the struggle despite this fact.

Part of our fear of death lies precisely in this story of Sisyphus. We fear that the struggle of our life, a struggle in which we never have time enough or love enough, will ultimately remain unfinished. We fear being useless. The older we get, the more certain we are that we have not completed what we intended. Indeed, as time goes on, the more we fear that our death will render our life like that of Sisyphus: the boulder will elude our grasp at the last.

So it is worthwhile to note that Eddie begins without fear. Fear, pain, worry: all are being swallowed up as he falls headlong into the sea. "This is he who came by water and blood… not by water alone, but by water and blood" (1 John 5:6). Fear impedes understanding. He must be free of fear if he would be able to hear what is said to him. He must hear in order to learn. But there is more.

Because we are "saved through water" (1 Peter 3:20), Eddie is plunged into water, for "the heavens existed of old and earth was formed out of water and through water by the word of God" (2 Pet 3:5). Fear is a kind of death. He is not only being freed of fear, he is also being reborn into his new life. Like any new-born child, he has much to learn.

The Sound of Silence

Some things change, some things do not. Eddie awakens from his plunge into the sea to find he is limber as a babe. His physical pain is gone, but he is still on Ruby Pier. He quickly encounters his first person: the Blue Man.

The Blue Man carries this first conversation, reading Eddie's mind and answering his questions as they arise. How is it possible for the Blue Man to accomplish this feat? "Eye hath not seen, nor ear heard, neither hath it entered into the heart of man, what things God hath prepared for those who love Him." (1 Corinthians 2:9). The Blue Man must have these skills in order to answer Eddie's questions. Why? Because God has given Eddie the gift of silence.

> "It is good to wait with silence for the salvation of God. It is good for a man, when he hath borne the yoke from his youth. He shall sit solitary, and hold his peace: because he hath taken it up upon himself. He shall put his mouth in the dust; there may be hope."
> *Lamentations 3:26-29*

Eddie is rendered silent because he needs to listen. "Let the islands keep silent before me and the nations take new strength; let them come near, then speak, let us come near to judgment together" (Isaiah 41:1). During the long years of his life, Eddie has made himself an island, cut himself off from others. He needs to reconnect. But to do that, he needs to listen. Eddie and the Blue Man are each given the gifts necessary to accomplish what is set before them.

Once Eddie understands his role in the Blue Man's life, or rather, in his death, he expects only one thing: judgement. Notice how he reacts. He squares his body. He prepares for what is coming. He does not reject the truth of his complicity or hide behind the fact that he was a child, completely unaware of what he had done. Rather, he accepts the truth set before him, and he readies himself for judgment. Eddie's readiness to accept responsibility for his actions is precisely why Eddie is worthy of mercy.

Instead of wreaking justice upon him, the Blue Man merely confirms what he has already shown by his actions. He had begun with quiet conversation and a warm touch. Now he tells Eddie that he has entered into the first step of heaven. Eddie begins to discover the truth: he is the student. He will meet five people, who will each serve as teachers, helping him to come to a deeper understanding of himself, a deeper understanding of God. He will learn that with God, "mercy triumphs over justice" (James 2:13). The Blue Man is the first example of this truth.

Communion

Eddie's communion with God's messengers, his ability to communicate what he needs to say, grows over time. As we will discover later, Eddie spent some of his life hiding from God, and the rest thinking he had gone unnoticed. This poor relationship with God is mirrored in his poor relationship with his father. His image of God is built in part on his image of his own father – a man who had harsh, unforgiving standards. Eddie had good reason to think God and his father had common goals for him.

After all, his father had wanted Eddie to work at Ruby Pier, he had always wanted his son to follow him in his work. Since Eddie *had*, in fact, lived exactly this life despite the fact that he had always wanted to leave that place, Eddie concludes that this must have been God's will. Eddie unconsciously assumes that God must be much like his father. From this point of view, his father had become, in a certain sense, a prophet of God; Eddie's own life was the evidence.

Thus, the Blue Man's poor relationship with his own father, the poverty that drove him to the silver nitrate and, eventually the freak show, mirrored Eddie's stormy family relationship.

God's gifts transform. By helping us understand what happened in our own life, we become prepared to share in His life. And that life, ultimately, is heaven: sharing in the divine life of love.

> We cannot accept an expensive gift when our hands are full of cheap baubles. We must empty our hands so as to grasp the rich gift that is offered.

The Blue Man is uniquely suited to introduce Eddie to heaven. Eddie spent the years following his wife's death in his own self-created poverty. He lived a poverty of friendship, a poverty of human acquaintance. During his life, the Blue Man also lived this poverty of loneliness. His version of Ruby Pier or at least what Eddie can see of his version of Ruby Pier, is empty save for the two of them. "This is not your heaven, this is mine," says the Blue Man.

But is that all there is to heaven? Do each of us wander about in our own created world? It hardly seems possible. We are each made for intimate communion with God. God desires intimate communion with each person. If we are in His image and likeness - if heaven restores all that Adam lost - then our desire for communion would be like unto God's. We would desire communion with all the persons who have ever lived.

The Blue Man gives us the hint that there is, in fact, more: "Heaven itself has many steps. This, for me, is the second. And for you, the first." Further, the lesson that he has for Eddie tells us that there is more, a reality that Eddie is not yet prepared to see: "No life is a waste... The only time we waste is the time we spend thinking we are alone."

He already knows what Eddie is just learning. "If I ascend into heaven, thou art there; if I descend into Sheol, thou art there. If I take my wings early in the morning and dwell in the uttermost parts of the sea, even there also shall thy hand lead me, and thy right hand shall hold me" (Psalm 139:8-10). God does not abandon us. Those who live out in their beings the life of God likewise do not abandon others.

Slowly, as the story unfolds, Eddie becomes aware of more and more people. By the end of the story, he will be able to see all the people on Ruby Pier, all who have ever gone or ever will go. He will know them and wait for them, watching them with love, for "we have over us a great cloud of witnesses" (Hebrews 12:1).

All lives interconnect, even the lives of people we barely knew, even the lives of strangers. We are all one body. One part of the body cannot say to another, "I do not need you." Indeed, it is quite the reverse: "if one member suffer anything, all the members suffer with it, or if one member glory, all the members rejoice with it" (1 Corinthians 12:26).

Those in heaven need to witness and assist precisely because they live God's life now, and this is part of what God does for us. That is why "Eddie felt everything the Blue Man had felt in his life rushing into him, swimming in his body, the loneliness, the shame, the nervousness, the heart attack." He is getting a lesson in compassion, a word that means "to suffer with."

Notice this. The Blue Man does not shield him from suffering, he allows Eddie to participate in the suffering he felt. And in that participation, "the drawer [is] closed," for the Blue Man did not just suffer, he was also honored. His skin becomes beautiful and unblemished as he steps towards his own gravesite.

The Blue Man accepted the poverty his skin imposed on him, and in that acceptance, he is perfected. The poverty of the grave has taught him how to accept the poverty he lived, the poverty he lived in turn prepared him for heaven's riches. We cannot accept an expensive gift when our hands are full of cheap baubles. We must empty our hands so as to grasp the rich gift that is offered. Like the Prodigal Son, we can receive rings for our fingers only if our hands are empty, we can receive shoes only if we are unshod (Luke 15).

This is the reason we must learn the poverty of death. We give up everything, even our bodies, so that we may receive everything, even our bodies, back anew, "It is sown in dishonour, it shall rise in glory, it is sown in weakness, it shall rise in power." (1 Corinthians 15:43). It is the only way to get home.

Heavenly Habits

Prudence

When Eddie recognized the mechanical problem involved in Freddie's Free Fall, when he dove beneath the ride in his attempt to save a young girl's life at the risk of his own, he was just being prudent.

We often have a mistaken understanding of prudence. We think of prudent people as those who avoid risk, those who work at self-preservation in a manner that almost verges on the selfish. But this kind of a man is exactly the opposite of a prudent man. In fact, if we do evil, or permits evil to happen through inaction, we are being imprudent.

A prudent man accurately assesses the reality of what is happening around him and acts to maintain or improve the good that he sees. As the entire crowd saw the disaster at the ride unfolding, only Eddie was able to accurately assess what had happened. He alone grasped the reality of the situation. In consequence, as the crowd surged and knocked the young girl off her feet and into danger, only Eddie was prepared to act immediately and decisively to save her.

He alone could act so quickly because he alone understood exactly what had gone wrong. Eddie was a prudent man.

> A prudent man accurately assesses the reality of what is happening around him and acts to maintain or improve the good that he sees.

Prudence is grounded in thorough knowledge and understanding of the world: the prudent man suffers no illusions either for good or ill. He knows the reality. But we should be careful here. Knowledge is not by itself enough to create prudence. The knowledge must be acted on.

Eddie alone was willing to close down rides if the tracks weren't greased, if the brakes weren't checked. He knew his responsibilities and refused to shirk them, even when others shirked theirs. He acted on reality. Prudence is both knowledge and action: accurate vision, timely action.

Long years with the rides had made this prudence a habit with him. He had learned the rhythms of the world of Ruby Pier. He knew it intimately, knew it so well that he could sometimes just *hear* when things were right or wrong.

Wisdom

And this is another critical characteristic of the prudent man. He can stand still and listen. As the head maintenance man, Eddie discovered how to learn by listening, he learned to act on what he heard. Eddie's life at Ruby Pier had trained him to be wise, for prudence is simply wisdom in action. Wisdom is a marvelous word, for it describes most exactly what it means to be prudent. To discover why this is so, we must study the word more closely.

The Germans have two words for knowledge: *kennen* and *wissen. Kennen* refers to book knowledge; it is an intellectual, theoretical knowledge that I may or may not be able to apply in a given situation. But *wissen* is knowledge that is based in experience and bred in the bone.

Wisdom is actually two words in one: wis-dom. *Wis* means "knowing the right way of doing a thing" and *dom* means "judgement." To *wis* something is to know it intimately, as a lover knows his love.

But what of *dom*? The word *dom* is simply a short form of the word *doom*. *Doom* does not mean what we think. When we speak of Doom's Day, or the Book of Doom, we are using the ancient words for Judgement Day and the Book of Judgement. When we speak of a *kingdom*, we are speaking of the geographical area subject to a king's judgement. *Doom* does not mean "death" or "punishment." It means "judgment."

Thus, when we say a man or woman possesses *wisdom*, we mean that man or woman judges rightly about how to do things. *Prudence* recognizes the reality and acts in accordance with it, *wisdom* correctly judges what the right action is.

Docility

As the rides of Ruby Pier had taught Eddie, wisdom requires silence, the ability to be still and learn from what is seen around us. And that's what he often did: just stand and listen. His prudence and his wisdom were grounded in his docility, his willingness to be silent and listen. This stillness, this willingness to learn from what surrounds us, is the true meaning of docility. But here is yet another word that is misunderstood. We often think that docility involves being a doormat, a shrinking violet. It really means nothing of the sort.

> "It ain't braggin' if you can do it."
> *Mark Twain*

The docile man is wise because the docile man knows his own abilities. "It ain't braggin' if you can do it," Mark Twain liked to say, and this sums up the docile man. He knows when he can accomplish what he sets out to do. He knows when he is in over his head. Either way, he acts in accordance with the reality of his own abilities. Docility is naturally a component of prudence – without docility, we cannot be prudent, without prudence, we cannot be wise.

Eddie discovers that all who enter heaven are unable to speak at first: the virtue of docility, the silence of observation, is enforced on us. Just as Eddie could stand still and hear when things went wrong with the rides, so this enforced silence allowed him to stand still and hear the things that went wrong in his life. He had learned docility, prudence and wisdom in his life at Ruby's Pier. Now he needed to use and sharpen those skills in a new place: heaven.

If we are to enter heaven, we must be wise, that is, we must have trained in prudence and in docility. Docility helps us quiet ourselves so we can truly observe reality, and truly act in accordance with it. Docility leads to prudence, prudence leads to wisdom. In heaven, all illusion is stripped away. "We see now through a mirror, dimly, but there face to face. Now I know in part, but then I shall know even as I am known" (1 Corinthians 13:12). We prepare for heaven by leaving the false wealth of our illusions behind here.

Poverty

We may summarize this way. The wise man is docile. He makes himself still, he listens to the world. He thereby makes himself prudent, discerning the reality and readying himself for right action. In the moment of decision, he lives wisdom: deciding how to judge rightly concerning both the act and the moment in which to act.

For every wise man, the ultimate object of his docile, prudent wisdom is preparation: he prepares for the inevitable by training for it. The wise man constantly chooses poverty, so that death is no shock, so that the loss of the body is the only burden the wise man must carry through death's narrow door.

Questions for Discussion

1. Why did Eddie meet the Blue Man and not his own father?

2. The phrase "wouldn't be prudent" is a source of comic relief in some circles. How would you explain prudence to someone who didn't understand it?

3. How is docility a kind of poverty?

4. Given the links that have been made here, can you comment on some deeper, unspoken reasons people might have for avoiding poverty? Avoiding the poor? Compare and contrast the lived examples of those who avoid the poor and poverty and those who embrace both. Who is more likely to be teacher, and who is more likely to be taught?

Scriptures for Contemplation

Exodus 23:3 – Do not favor a poor man.
Exodus 23:6 – Do not ignore a poor man.
Leviticus 23:22 – How to remember the poor.

Further reading

The Four Cardinal Virtues by Josef Pieper
The Many Faces of Virtue by Donald DeMarco

The Second Person: The Captain

The Battlefield

Eddie has learned the first lesson. He must now enter his second encounter, the encounter at the banyan tree. This encounter at the tree describes the beginning of his personal fall from grace, for this is how he views his injury (Genesis 3).

Just as the first encounter began with a kind of baptism, as he plunged into the sea only to find himself "reborn" at Ruby's Pier, this second encounter also begins with a baptism as the rain pours down upon his head. But though the first baptism emphasized re-birth, here a different aspect is emphasized: "For we are buried together with Him by baptism into death…" (Romans 6:4).

As Eddie crawls through the mud and the pouring rain, he encounters his own dogtags on a rifle: the military symbol signifying a soldier's grave. But the death this rifle signifies is not the physical death he experienced under Freddie's Free Fall, rather, it is the spiritual death he lived as a result of his war injury. Because of that injury, he withdrew into himself, he began walling himself off from the world. Just as the physical injury never really healed, the wound this physical injury inflicted on his soul never really healed.

> They killed Him, hanging Him upon a tree.
> *Acts 10:39*

Eddie has to rise above this wound. "They killed Him, hanging Him upon a tree" (Acts 10:39). He climbs a tree to meet the Captain. And there, in the branches of the banyan tree, the Captain asks the question that is one of the keys to understanding Eddie's life: "Do you still juggle?"

Eddie was smart, skilled, capable. Like a great juggler, he could work around anything - a broken amusement park ride, bad food, captivity, even being worked to death in a coal mine. When he and the Captain were captured during the war, he was the one who created the opportunity for their escape: he juggled.

But where his physical skills flourished, his spiritual skills did not. His captivity had begun with hope in God and expectation of escape. As a prisoner, his hope in God died when the guards killed his friend. He had spent months, even years learning how to become mechanically adept, how to work around the physical obstacles life threw at him. He had spent no time at all learning how to become spiritually adept, learning how to work around the spiritual obstacles life threw at him.

Thus, his hope of physical escape from captivity never left him, but his hope of spiritual escape did. His refusal to give up hope in his own physical abilities made successful escape from imprisonment possible, but it was exactly his inability to hold onto spiritual hope that made his life after the escape unbearable. Because of this, his body left prison, but his soul never did.

Deeper into the Mystery

War is about betrayal and sacrifice. The first begets war, the second stops it. But either way, the reality of both life and death permeate it. Eddie freed himself and his friends from his captors, but he surrendered to his wounds.

The Captain made one promise: no one gets left behind. This is, in part, a re-phrasing of what the Blue Man had taught Eddie: no one is ever alone. But it is not just a simple re-phrasing: there is more. If I am in a terrible situation, it is good to know that someone chooses to stay with me. It is better to know that this same someone will take me out of the situation.

"No one gets left behind." This was a promise that expanded upon the Blue Man's promise. The Blue Man said the only time we waste is the time we spend thinking we are alone. The Captain's promise not only told Eddie that he would not be alone, but also that he would be free. No matter what else might happen, he and his friends would not be left behind to languish.

But why is this important? What's wrong with being forever alone?

The answer is very simple. We are each persons. A person is a creature made for intimate communion, in fact, the ability to partake of intimate communion is the distinguishing mark of a person. Indeed, it is impossible to be a person without being in some kind of communion with another person. The very word "communion" demands two persons, while the word "person" demands communion: trying to speak of a person in eternal isolation is almost nonsensical, like trying to describe a square circle. It can't be done.

> Trying to speak of a person in eternal isolation is almost nonsensical, like trying to describe a square circle. It can't be done.

Because we are persons, each of us is made for communion, for life with other persons. "It is not good for man to be alone..." (Genesis 2:18). But If other people make up my salvation, if they save me from the loneliness that is my private hell, then their presence must be acknowledged or there is no communion. In short, if we are never alone, then we are responsible for each other. The Captain knew this.

Through his death, the Captain accomplished exactly the physical salvation that he had always promised Eddie. Paradoxically, however, because Eddie dwelt on the sacrifices made, he was spiritually left behind. The bullet stayed in him while the rest of the world moved on. But he was not just left behind. It was worse - he chose to remain behind. He dwelt on the wound, and stopped believing in the possibility of escape from the consequences of the wound.

Eddie forgot that every promise carries a price. If no one is to be left behind, if no one is to be left alone, then everyone must endure more hardship in order to make that escape from solitude possible. "Greater love than this has no man, that he lay down his life for his friends" (John 15:13).

The Price of a Promise

Again, poverty is something all of us encounter, whether physically, emotionally, or spiritually. But sacrifice is more than simply experiencing poverty: it is being willing to choose poverty in order to promote someone else's good.

The Blue Man introduced Eddie to the concept. He lived his poverty, but he came to know that he was not alone. His life served as a model for Eddie. The Captain went deeper. He imposed a poverty on Eddie so that both he and Eddie could keep their promises.

The Captain knew what Eddie did not. He understood the price that had to be paid. Thus, the landmine he triggered was a price he willingly accepted in order to keep his promise to his men, his friends. He walked the path first because he had promised them the path would be safe, and he intended to make sure it was. Because the Captain kept his promise, God granted Eddie's promise, the prayer Eddie invoked every night before he lost faith in God: Eddie gained safe harbor again in Marguerite's arms. The Captain allowed the war to ravage his own body in order to assure Eddie's survival.

The Captain's bullet forced Eddie to face the reality of sacrifice. Eddie had promised to return to Marguerite. Without the

Captain's intervention, he would not have been able to accomplish it. It is here in the tree that Eddie realizes what actually happened: the life-long physical pain he suffered was not something he chose at the moment he was shot, rather, he had chosen it when he enlisted, he had chosen it when he danced at the Stardust Bandshell that last night with Marguerite. Though he never spoke the words aloud, he had made her a promise to return. The price of that promise was the bullet in his leg.

Eddie did not realize he had chosen such an enormous price, but this is often the way with each of us. When we make our vows at the altar, do we really understand what we are voluntarily sacrificing? When we beget children, when we birth children, do we really understand all the implications of that choice?

Of course not. Any choice of real substance includes choosing something beyond ourselves. God calls us to communion to Himself. If we choose to embrace His offer, we have chosen something whose consequences we cannot fully see or understand. Our individual choices in this life, the choices whose ultimate consequences are beyond our perception, these are the ways in which we get practice in how to make that most important eternal choice. "I call heaven and earth to witness this day, that I have set before you life and death, the blessing and the curse. Choose life, that both thou and thy seed may live" (Deuteronomy 30:19).

> I call heaven and earth to witness this day,
> that I have set before you life and death,
> the blessing and the curse. Choose life,
> that both thou and thy seed may live"
> *Deuteronomy 30:19*

This is where poverty truly begins to be embraced. In the enormously wonderful story that J.R.R. Tolkien gives us in his Ring trilogy, Frodo sees his responsibility and says, "I will take the Ring, though I do not know the way." As a result of that choice, everything is taken from him except the selfless love of his friend.

That is how it is with each of us. I see a responsibility. I face the fact that this responsibility waits on but a word from me to become mine, and I dimly know that this responsibility will change me beyond what I know of myself, beyond even what I know of my own capabilities. Do I choose it? And when I do, do I stand by my choice, no matter the cost?

Some stand hard upon the challenge. "Faithless is he that says farewell when the road darkens," asserts the dwarf Gimli in Tolkien's work. But Elrond replies, "Maybe, but let him not vow to walk in the dark, who has not seen the nightfall." Gimli knows that "Sworn word may strengthen quaking heart," but Elrond knows such words can also break it.

Like Frodo, Eddie had the opportunity to embrace all the consequences of his decision. Unlike Frodo, he mourned for what he had lost to such an extent that his life became a silent agony for him.

This is the war that each of us fight within ourselves. When unforeseen difficulty arises, when our initial choice demands of us a poverty that we did not foresee, when the poverty we unknowingly chose strikes at the heart of what we cling to, what will we do?

The prudent man accurately assesses reality, but being finite, even he cannot avoid this choice. There is only one way to prepare.

What is to be Done?

If we live as one already accommodated to death, the fight is over in an instant. The wise man knows he must accept poverty sometime. Now is as good a time as any.

The rest of us are not so sanguine about it. We fight, we struggle to hold onto something which is not eternal. The war that

Eddie had fought within himself all his long years, the war over whether or not to accept the sacrifice he made in order to live life with his beloved, that war finally came to the surface here in the banyan tree.

He began to beat the Captain. The Captain turned not his cheek (Matthew 5:39). Eddie fought the war within himself by raging upon the Captain's body. The Captain understood that this war must be fought, and, for the second time, he permitted his body to become the battleground.

Sacrifice always involves this war, this combat that tears at our souls and forces us to choose between our comfort and someone else's joy. Only the Captain, a military man who trained his whole life towards living sacrifice, could fully understand its demands.

Again, because sacrifice is part of every life, the wise man prepares for it, discerns how to make the most of it. Ultimately, we discover how to win the battle raging within our souls: we must become centered on those around us and not on ourselves.

Like the death for which it prepares us, living a life in a way that accommodates the inevitable changes the way we live. The Zen masters insist the best way to defeat an enemy is to bend before him. Abraham Lincoln, a great student of the Bible, said he destroyed his enemies by making them his friends.

The wise man befriends sacrifice, turns it into a constant companion, chooses it, practices it, lives it, over and over again, so that necessary sacrifices are more easily absorbed and are finally no real sacrifice at all. Each decision to accept deeper poverty becomes another joy, another gift to those in need, the attainment of a goal that we strive mightily to reach. When sacrifice changes from an obstacle to a goal, nothing can shake life's even keel.

Because the Captain knows this, he sees a world Eddie can only begin to glimpse after he has forgiven the Captain: a world without war.

It is beautiful.

Heavenly Habits

Faith

We can now see a larger symmetry to the themes being brought forward. Eddie's first encounter ultimately centered around a lack of faith. Both Eddie and the Blue Man lacked it during their lives. The second encounter was just the opposite. The Captain kept faith. That is what allowed him to sacrifice.

This word, "faith," causes no end of problems for us. Many people throw it around as if everyone knows what it means, but most of us do not. We think of faith only in terms of gift. Like any gift, it seems to be undefined, ethereal, untouchable: there is a wall of wrapping paper and ribbons that separates it from us and the world. Thinking of faith primarily in terms of "gift" creates all kinds of problems.

For instance, a gift is something our intellects cannot really touch. When we are given a gift, we don't know what is in the pretty box or the handsome bag until it is revealed. Gifts always begin as something outside of our experience, something extrinsic to what we are and where we are, they are unexpected and therefore beyond our thoughts.

Thus, when we think of faith primarily in terms of "gift," we think of it as something separate from intellect. That is why the word "faith" often brings to mind a blind man groping in the dark, or more likely, a sighted man ignoring clearly revealed facts in favor of some invisible knowledge only he can discern, a knowledge we cannot access.

This gift-based approach to faith is based in misunderstanding. Faith is not blind. It is not based on hidden or invisible knowledge, though it is perfectly true that "faith is the substance of things hoped for, the evidence of things not seen" (Hebrews 11:1). But too often we emphasize the "things not seen" at the expense of the *evidence*. In fact, faith is built on facts, facts easily accessible and agreed upon. Like every branch of knowledge, faith is evidence-based.

Take one example of an act of faith. If I enter a restaurant, study the menu and order breakfast, I have performed an act of faith. I have faith that the order will be taken correctly by the waitress. I have faith the cook will prepare a good breakfast. That is why I decided to enter the restaurant and order the meal in the first place – I had faith this place could accomplish what the facts indicated.

> Faith is built on facts, facts easily accessible and agreed upon. Like every branch of knowledge, faith is evidence-based.

What are these facts? Outside, a sign indicates it is a restaurant. Inside, it has tables set for a meal. Each table carries a menu describing different meals. The people who work in it talk about food and ask me what I want to eat. The tantalizing odor of well-cooked food wafts in from behind two swinging doors that lead to another room (I have faith that it is the kitchen). These facts comprise the evidence that I might, in fact, get a good meal here. So, I ask in faith, and I receive a meal.

Is it a good meal? That is the only fact I don't know. Perhaps I have been here before, but that hardly matters. Even if I have been to this restaurant before and enjoyed the meals, the cook might be having a bad day today. Perhaps today's meal will not be as good as I am used to or as good as I hoped. But I have good reason for believing that this will not be the case, or I would not sit down and order. The evidence not seen - the meal itself - that is faith's object.

My act of faith was not an act of blindness. It was based on evidence. The object of my act of faith was the only thing I did not see. I did not see the meal before I chose it, before I tasted it, but I had sufficient evidence to choose it.

Blind faith is altogether different. If I saw a building with a sign that said "Hardware", if I entered and observed bins filled with nuts and bolts, walls festooned with tools, if I heard the clerk discussing how to install a kitchen faucet, and if I turned to that clerk and asked for two eggs over easy, with a side of bacon and a glass of orange juice, then I would have exhibited blind faith. After all, I have no evidence the store or the clerk is prepared to deal with this request. Indeed, all the evidence is against it. I am operating on some hidden knowledge or hidden urging that you cannot comprehend, an urging that even I may not clearly comprehend. If I actually received what I ordered in that hardware store, I would be face-to-face with a miracle.

Faith in God is very much like my faith in the restaurant. "The heavens show forth the glory of God and the firmament declares the work of His hands" (Psalm 19:1). That is, I can look at the natural world around me and see that it is good (Genesis 1). I have the evidence of the ordered universe that God exists and the He rewards those who seek Him (Hebrews 11:6).

I also have the evidence of men who testify to the goodness of God: these are the Hebrew prophets and apostles. The very existence of the world tells me God loves me so much that an entire universe was built to care for my needs. The prophets and apostles tell me He loves me so much, He even entered the world in the flesh of a man in order to minister to my needs.

> The Captain had faith.
> Eddie and the Blue Man did not.

But there is even more. These men recorded the events of history and the words of His mouth so that I can know God Himself testified to the same thing. He loves me. He intends my good. He will accomplish it, for "no word shall be impossible with God" (Luke 1:37)

I did not see Him walk in Jerusalem. When I ordered breakfast, I did not see the eggs and ham either, not until the proper time to see them had arrived and everything was prepared. The evidence I have been given - the world, the history - is enough for me. I am content to wait; not in blind faith, but with informed faith, using the facts that God Himself gives me through the world, the prophets and the Word.

We sacrifice our money at the fast-food counter because we have faith that we will receive food worthy of the sacrifice. The Captain sacrificed his life for his men because he had faith that such sacrifice was worthwhile. But the Blue Man and Eddie had lost faith, so they were not prepared to sacrifice. They did not believe there could be adequate recompense for what they had lost.

Hope

The Blue Man originally had faith in the doctor's silver nitrate solution. He had every reason to believe the doctor would help him, that the doctor's remedy would, in fact, help his nerves. When it did not help him, he did not initially lose faith – he did not throw the medicine away – rather, he began to lose hope.

Here again we have met a word that we do not understand as well as we think we do. There is a reason for that. We don't understand hope because we don't understand the relationship between faith and hope.

I have faith in persons. For instance, when I entered the restaurant, the evidence inside and out pointed to a person with a plan.

If faith is based on the facts of a situation, that is, if it is based on what we know about a person's ability to plan and care for others, then hope is based on the message the person has for us. I have faith in the people who run the restaurant, I believe they are capable even though I might never have been in that restaurant before. The very fact that the business exists indicates the people within have some minimum level of capability.

My hope that I will receive a good meal comes from their message. These capable people tell me they can prepare a good meal. Because of the evidence of their plan, I act in faith. Because of the evidence of their message, I have hope that my hunger will soon be satisfied. Faith is based on the facts of who a person is, the knowledge that someone is reliable. Hope is based on the content of what this reliable person tells me.

The Blue Man began with faith in the doctor, hope in the doctor's message. His faith and hope were misplaced. The Blue Man's faith and hope were, at first, unshakeable. But as he took the doctor's medicine and noticed no change in his nervous condition, the Blue Man began to lose hope.

> I have faith in reliable persons.
> I have hope based on the message the
> reliable person has for me.

He still had faith in the doctor and the doctor's advice, but he had lost faith in his own ability to follow that advice correctly, and he began to lose hope that the message was true. He continued using the medicine, but at greater and greater dosages. He had more faith in the doctor than he had in himself. As he slowly began to realize the awful results of the treatment, he lost both faith and hope. As a result, he lived in a friendless, hopeless world.

Eddie went through a similar process. He had faith in the Captain. The Captain was a life-long military man. He was reliable. The Captain said no one would be left behind, so Eddie had hope.

Even though the Captain disappeared, Eddie could see that he had been saved, so he kept his faith in the Captain.

Likewise, Eddie began with faith in God. He believed God to be reliable. God tells us that He will always care for us, so that gave Eddie hope. But he lost faith in God because he could not understand what he saw, he could not correlate the fact of his friend's death with the idea that God cares for us, or with the idea that God could still bring good out of such a terrible loss. From Eddie's point of view, God appeared to be unreliable. His hope died when his faith died.

Though Eddie kept faith in the Captain, and had hope in the Captain's promise, though Eddie had faith in his own abilities (juggling) and therefore hope of escape, his ultimate hope was gone. He saw the evil done to his friend in the mines and lost the ability to see past the evil, to put faith into the possibility that every evil can be turned to good. As a consequence, when evil struck him in its turn (the Captain's bullet in his leg), he had no source of hope. He saw nothing but a lifetime of pain.

Though God can bring good out of any evil, Eddie no longer believed it. The Captain had disappeared. The doctors, who merited little faith, did not have a hope-filled message. They told him nothing more could be done.

Eddie was alone. He had no one who could be trusted, no one who could give him a message worthy of hope. All Eddie had was pain and a cane.

Heaven requires faith in God and hope in the message He provides. The Blue Man and the Captain lay the groundwork to help Eddie understand why he should never have surrendered faith or hope in God.

God does not leave us alone. Even better, God has always had a plan: no one gets left behind. We are meant to acknowledge these facts, acknowledge Him and the people He sends, by enduring sacrifices for others. Faith in God, hope in His message, these are based in the fact that we will not be left alone or behind; these facts, in turn, require us to embrace sacrifice so that all may be saved.

Questions for Discussion

1. Why did Eddie meet the Captain in the banyan tree and not Rabozzo?

2. To say "Faith is a gift" describes how I receive it, but the phrase does not tell me what it is. Why is it more accurate to say "Faith is power" or "Faith is knowledge"?

3. How would you explain the difference between faith and hope to someone who has questions about these two habits?

4. A virtue is defined as a "good habit that is in harmony with our human nature." Why is this a useful way to talk about virtues? What does it imply about our ability to grow in virtue?

Scriptures for Contemplation

Luke 1:1-4 – Luke swears others met God enfleshed.
2 Tim 1:8-12 – Paul swears he met God in the flesh.
1 John 1:1-4 – John swears he met God in the flesh.

Further reading

Faith, Hope, Love by Josef Pieper
The Heart of Virtue by Donald DeMarco

The Third Person:
Ruby

The Diner

As Eddie prepares for his third person, he walks through the mountains in ankle-deep snow that is neither "cold nor wet." The mountain has long been associated with the journey to meet God. Just as the Spirit and the Son bring us to the Father, so the encounters with the Blue Man and the Captain have now brought Eddie to an encounter with his own father.

The baptismal waters, which were first sea and rain, have now become "ankle-deep" snow. Prior to his crucifixion and ascension into heaven to meet the Father, Jesus washed the feet of his disciples and celebrated the Passover meal with them (John 13:5-12). Similarly, before Eddie can meet the truth about his own father, about the relationship he has with him, his feet must be washed. Only then can he begin his encounter with the third person, outside a diner.

Meals are important. After Jesus taught the crowds, He fed them, although it required a miracle to accomplish the task and much grumbling on the part of the apostles (Mark 6:35-44). Likewise, before He offered Himself on the Cross, He first offered His apostles the meal. There is a reason for this. Those who begin their communion through sacrifice for one another grow in their communion through the shared meal, for the meal is a kind of sacrifice.

> Christ washed the apostles' feet before the Last Supper. Eddie walks through ankle-deep snow before his encounter at the diner.

At each meal, we surrender part of what lies before us to the other, for the enjoyment and good of the other. But a shared meal is not just sacrifice. It is also a common taking of comfort, it is the fulfillment of the need for which sacrifice is made. When we feast together, we acknowledge both each other's sacrifice and we mutually fulfill the hunger we endured because of our earlier sacrifice.

Eddie's inability to communicate with his father in this place of shared meals is a sign of the strain between them. Scripture tells us over and over that the sins of the father are visited upon the sons down to the third and fourth generation. Many who read this find it hard to accept. How can God be this vengeful, this vindictive? Like death, the answer is not something we like to face. You see, the problem is not really with God. It is with us.

Like Father, Like Son

We know that children are like their parents. Parents who are kind, thoughtful, pious, tend to have children who are kind, thoughtful, pious. Parents who are vicious, impious and cruel are likely to have children who are like them. God helps us understand what it means to be made in His image and likeness by allowing us to be formed into the image and likeness of our human parents. The difference between our human parents and our divine Father lies only in this: God cares for us and our needs in ways more loving, more attentive, than any human parent could.

At times, we have trouble believing this. How can God be taking care of me while my father is beating me? While my family is starving? While my child is dying?

We must remember that God made each person a free agent. The freedom He grants us is like unto His own freedom, with one exception. He is wise enough, powerful enough to never be a slave. We who are merely finite and ignorant, we can foolishly give away our freedom and become slaves.

The moment we choose slavery, we choose to throw away our likeness to God. We reject Him. We reject the similarities between our human nature and the one divine nature.

That decision to accept slavery and reject freedom is made at the moment we deliberately harm each other. It is easy to see why.

God is the source of life and freedom. The rejection of freedom is a rejection of God. In our rejection of God, we attack His image. Since we are each an image of God, rejecting God means we necessarily attack each other.

There is good news. God's goodness is more powerful than our evil. Since He is infinitely good, he can take the finite evils we wreak upon one another and bring an even greater good out of them.

There is bad news. Because we are not too bright, transforming the evil we commit into a good we can understand takes time. It takes time for us to understand what happened, both for evil and for good. It also takes time for us to accept the transformation. The acceptance is the hard part.

Eddie needs to see his father through an adult lens. He has to understand that his father struggled through the same human life, through the same kinds of difficulties, he struggled through. That is why Eddie's questions to Ruby are so important.

He begins by asking if he can talk to God. God is our Father. He is the one with whom we are made to commune. When Ruby assures him he can, Eddie declares for the first time his desire to go back to his old life. Why? Because he knows deep in his heart what is coming.

In our rejection of God, we attack His image. Since we are each an image of God, rejecting God means we necessarily attack each other.

His old life was filled with pain, regret, loneliness – but even this is preferable to being transformed. It is hard to want what you do not know or fully understand. The devil you know is preferable.

Eddie knows that making peace with himself involves making peace with his father, for he had become his father in most ways. Though he hated the idea of working at the pier, though he hated the silence and the beatings he received from his father, still he allowed himself to live as his father had. His father's life had trapped him precisely because Eddie knew his life should in some way mirror his father. This is hard to understand. Perhaps we can say it another way.

Though Eddie was a unique and unrepeatable individual who glorified God in a unique and unrepeatable way, still he understood in his gut that he was made in the image and likeness of his father. His relationship with his human father was one of silence. That is why his relationship with God was one of silence.

Eddie stopped talking to God when his friend was murdered. His father stopped talking to him when Eddie stopped his punch. Just as Eddie knew he was made in the image and likeness of his father, he understood on some level that his father was supposed to image God to him.

We all understand this connection on some level, but it is precisely because we do not think about it much that we do not think about it clearly. My father's virtues image God's life to me, but my father's sins image his rejection of God's life. As a child, it is easy to confuse the two. Eddie had. So do we.

The End of the Line

Eddie knew he worked "at the end of the line." He remembered his father as an old man, a man too old to have children. When he accepted his father's life, he became the man too old to have children as well. He thought his father's life was useless. He thought his own life was useless.

Because of the Blue Man, he knew that he was never alone. Because of the Captain, he discovered that this truth created another truth: we have a duty towards others that will involve sacrifice. Now this truth leads to part of Ruby's teaching: the sacrifices others make or refuse to make change our lives, even if we do not know anything concerning their decisions, even if we have never met the persons who made the sacrifices.

Ruby draws a circle, a lens in the baptismal snow. Eddie had crawled through a pouring rain prior to his encounter with the Captain. Now he sees Mickey Shea's transgression and his own father pursuing Mickey in the same kind of pouring rain, a sign of baptismal grace suspended in the point of decision. Eddie's father is justly angry. Should he kill Mickey for the outrages Mickey committed against his wife? It would be perfectly just to do so. But he sees Mickey try to commit suicide. Mickey is remorseful. So, should he save Mickey as an act of mercy to a man suffering from a complete loss of faith and hope: a man who is, in that moment, very much like Eddie?

It is in that moment, as he stands in the pouring rain on the edge of the sea, that Eddie's father lives out the image and likeness of God. His mercy triumphs over his justice. He lays down his life for his friend, even though his friend had sinned against him and against heaven. In this single act of mercy, Eddie recognizes the face of God. The veil is ripped away from his father's life, and he sees him with adult eyes.

In that moment, Eddie's father rescues not just Mickey, but his own son. In that moment, Eddie sees that he *is* made in the image and likeness of both God and of his father. As Ruby helps Eddie watch the scenes of his father's life unfold, his father's mercy is revealed to Eddie. Because he has seen his father live mercy, Eddie can now, in turn, show mercy to his father. "Amen, amen, I say to you, a son cannot do anything on his own, but only what he sees his father doing, for what he does, his son will do also." (John 5:19)

Like many of us, Mickey Shea was unable to accept the transformation that this act of mercy called him towards. Mickey's intemperance was not found just in his drink, it was found in his inability to accept the sacrifice made on his behalf. His father died for love of the man who sinned against him. To the very end, the man who was Mickey's friend, the man who was Eddie's father, called out to his family, his children, his friend. In that call, the silence between Eddie and his father was broken. The sins were expiated. "I live now not I, but Christ lives in me" (Galatians 2:20).

The anger Eddie felt towards his father was not directed towards his father's example as the head of maintenance on Ruby Pier. It was directed towards the sins his father had committed against the family. His father was not the reason he stayed at the pier. His anger was the reason. By staying at the pier, he was, in an unnamed, bewildered way, trying to fix what his father had broken in himself, in his family, in his life.

> Amen, amen, I say to you, a son cannot do anything on his own, but only what he sees his father doing, for what he does, his son will do also.
> *John 5:19*

Once he realized this, mercy could triumph over justice. To him who shows mercy, mercy is shown. His father was right to be angry with Mickey Shea and the outrages he committed. But he was also right to show forgiveness when Mickey's remorse for his own actions became strikingly clear. With this realization, Eddie could finally imitate his father, he could finally look at the outrages his father had committed, yet see the remorseful, lonely old man in the diner. He could finally turn to his father and say, "It's fixed."

And with that reparation, Ruby and his father could both follow the Blue Man, and move to their next step in heaven.

Heavenly Habits

Memory

Precisely because love lies at the center of all things, memory is of critical importance. After all, love is intimately tied to memory. The Captain hinted at this connection when he spoke of the little death that Adam experienced in sleep. When Adam awoke from that little death, he not only had a new day, "he had his yesterday" as well.

Wisdom, prudence, these depend on memories that are faithful. We must not only act upon reality, we must remember that we have acted, remember accurately what has happened in the past. That's why Ruby's story is so important. She knows the past better than Eddie does. She lived it.

Eddie's understanding of the past is strewn with errors in judgment and memory. He mis-judged his father in part because he did not know what really happened. The eyes of a child are the eyes of wonder because a child see all things new. Every sunrise and sunset brings new things to see, new and glorious connections to make, new opportunities for communion with others.

But precisely because everything is new, it is also impossible for a child to see each thing in its proper perspective to other things. The child races from the new-found flower to the new-found bug on the flower to the new-found rabbit amongst the flowers. The new-ness of each thing entrances, delights and distracts. Children cannot see the world as adults do. This is both an enormous virtue and a great tragedy.

As is true for each of us in our relationship with our own parents, Eddie was a child for much of his life with his father, and thus could not see the reality that lay before him. His father had to deal with issues that he did not, could not, burden his son with. As a result, Eddie's memories of his father did not accurately portray the reality. This lack of accurate memory interfered with his ability to love.

Justice, Part I

The opposite of love is not hate. The opposite of love is use. Justice insists that each person be treated as a person. But what does this mean? What is a person?

If we look at the first Persons, the three divine Persons of the Trinity, we see that the only thing that distinguishes each from the other is their relations. It is not immediately obvious why this would be true. But this is the key to understanding the importance of justice.

> The opposite of love is not hate.
> The opposite of love is use.

God is perfect. This word, "perfect", is hard for us to grasp, mostly because we aren't. But, despite our lack, we do know a little something about perfection. For instance, we know that existence is more perfect than non-existence. This is easy to demonstrate. Is it better to just have a mental picture of the perfect car, perfect meal, perfect clothes, or to actually *have* that car, that meal or those clothes? Clearly the existence of the perfect is better than the mere mental image.

Now, God has perfect knowledge of Himself. He always has had it. But if His knowledge of Himself is *perfect*, than that knowledge must have His own existence. He does. We call Him God the Son. God the Son is the perfect self-knowledge of the Father. We aren't used to thinking about God the Son this way, but we can see traces of this in the Scriptures: "In the beginning was the Word" (John 1:1).

Since God the Son is everything that God the Father knows about Himself, God the Father must give the Son everything He is. When we consider God the Son in this way, we see that God the Father pours Himself out completely into God the Son, holding nothing of Himself back. The Son has always existed, but He has also always found His origin in the Father.

As human beings, we aren't used to seeing such a thing, but it happens in the Godhead. We admit as much in the various creeds: God the Son is "*eternally begotten* of the Father, God from God, Light from Light, true God from true God, *begotten, not made*, one in being with the Father." In a sense, in this total gift that the Father makes of Himself to the Son, in this eternal begetting, He "takes care of" all the Son is and all the Son needs from all eternity to all eternity.

Now this total gift of self that the Father makes to the Son and that the Son makes to the Father is called the divine exchange of Persons. It is a perfect exchange. But there's that word again.

If the exchange of Persons is perfect, He must have His own existence. He does. He is God the Holy Spirit, the Person "who proceeds from the Father and the Son. With the Father and the Son He is worshipped and glorified." God the Father begets God the Son. The Father and the Son together "breathe" the Holy Spirit.

You have heard a lover say of his beloved, "You are the air I breathe!" This is what the Father and the Son say of the Spirit. That is why a human person might say it about a person he loves - we know we must live out in ourselves the absolute reality of God, in whose image and likeness we are. Even people who don't believe in God or understand the Trinity understand what it means to speak in this way.

Justice, Part II

And this is the key to understanding true justice. It is the key to understanding why the opposite of love is not hate. The opposite of love is use.

Each of the three Persons of the Godhead gives Himself away as gift to each of the other two Persons. Each Person cherishes, treasures, cares for the Divine Person who gives Himself. The only thing that distinguishes Father from Son and Son from Spirit is the relationship of love between them. Father begets Son, Son is begotten. Father and Son breathe forth Spirit, Spirit is breathed. Just as the persons of the Godhead are distinguished only by their relations, it is only our relationship to God that make us persons. Nothing more.

This is very important. We can now see that it is God who makes us persons. His call to each of us, His invitation to communion with Him – this is what makes us persons. As part of the invitation, He gives us everything we need to participate in the communion: He gives us our intellects, our wills, and the capacity to love as He loves. He makes us persons so we can share communion with the three Divine Persons.

If God did not call us into relationship with Himself, we would not be persons. Thus, if we refuse to relate to God, we attack our own personhood. Similarly, every time we refuse to relate to one another as images of God, we also attack our own personhood.

It is said that the one who sins destroys himself more effectively than he destroys the one sinned against. Now we can see why.

Justice means making sure another person receives his due. Justice is part of each person's *being*. It is an innate recognition of every relationship: you to me, me to you, each of us to God.

Someone who hates another person recognizes the relationship another person has with God: he simply despises that person and God for having such a relationship. Likewise, someone who has a good relationship with God hates to see the relationships of other persons damaged: he hates sin. Whether we hate a person (which is always sinful) or we hate an act (which may be in some cases justified), hatred at least has eyes for the truth. Hatred sees the relationships and acknowledges them, even if it is a negative acknowledgement. But with use, it is different.

When we treat someone else as a mere object to be used, we pretend that they have no relationship with God. That is, we pretend they are not persons at all. In short, using someone as an object is very much akin to denying God's existence. We deliberately blind ourselves to the intrinsic worth and beauty of the relationship, of the person. This is unjust.

Justice is the only habit that has the capacity to form our relations with other people. All the other virtues I may have are directed towards perfecting myself, but justice is directed towards perfecting my relationships with others.

And it is precisely because justice is about the relationship between myself and "other" that justice, in the strict sense, is not something that applies within a family. The child, in a sense, belongs to his parents, and parents belong to their children. The child is not the property of the parents as a chair or a car might be, rather, the child expresses in his own life aspects of his parents. The father feels, or should feel, towards the child the way he feels towards himself.

> Just as those who reject God's grace attack God's images, so those who reject themselves attack their own children.

God may have a relationship of justice towards us, but that is because we are "other" in respect to Him. Within Himself, between the three Persons of the Godhead, justice is not necessary. Similarly, the relationships within the family are not subject to strict justice precisely because these relationships are a very real, although very imperfect, mortal reflection of God's eternal inner life.

Unfortunately, the mirrors of our lives, both parents and children, are dimmed by sin. Sin is the willingness to use someone as an object. This explains quite a lot about many parent-child interactions.

Just as those who reject God's grace attack God's images, so those who reject themselves attack their children. Since each of us has aspects of ourselves that we do not like, it is no surprise to find that we as parents inevitably harm our children. This is what it means to say the sins of the parents are visited upon the children. God helps us grow towards Him, He helps us love our children, by insisting on justice. "For judgement without mercy is to him that hath not done mercy. But mercy triumphs over justice" (James 2:13).

Fortitude

In acting mercifully towards Mickey Shea, Eddie's father showed courage. Courage depends on many things. It begins with vulnerability. A man who cannot be hurt cannot be brave. Only those who can suffer injury can know bravery. And if I can suffer injury, then I can suffer death. Courage, then, is simply a readiness for death.

It is not a willingness to die, just a readiness to die. Prudence and justice precede fortitude – I must know why I fight before I will choose to fight. Courage describes my reaction to these assessments. I am courageous, I fight, when justice demands it. For this reason, courage is always a secondary virtue. It never stands by itself rather it requires the support of the other habits of life.

Courage is not foolhardiness: it assumes that a good reason exists to take the risks that are being taken. Courage is informed by prudence. In order to be courageous, I must have an accurate understanding of what I risk and an accurate understanding of what I gain or lose by taking or refusing the courageous act.

If justice gives each person what is due, then courage protects the gift from harm and makes sure the gift of justice is bestowed as it should be. If the gift to be protected is not worthy of protection, if the gift is not truly just, then taking risks on behalf of this false justice is not courage, it is foolhardiness.

As Josef Pieper points out in *The Four Cardinal Virtues*, "The brave man suffers injury not for its own sake, but rather as a means to preserve or to acquire a deeper, more essential intactness." We do not seek out injury if we rightly understand our relationship with God. Again, Pieper notes "Saint Cyprian, who was beheaded in 258 A.D. (it was a capital offense to practice the Catholic Faith), declared to the Consul Paternus: 'Our teaching forbids anyone to report himself.' " In justice, I am called to prevent others from attacking God or the living image of Him I find in an innocent man, even if that man is me.

Temperance

Every person struggles with sins, this is common knowledge. What we don't often consider is this: the sins we struggle with are sometimes not our own. Mickey Shea was virtuous in the sense that he was generous. He helped Eddie's father get a job at the pier; he gave freely of what little money he had in order to help with Eddie's birth.

But, as Montaigne notes, we are a patchwork quilt of emotions and drives. The person or thing we hate at this moment we may love in ten minutes. Emotions are wonderful and necessary to life. Like the finest spices, they garnish the living feast of our days. Without the joys and sorrows of life, our existence would be as insipid as the white of an egg (Job 6:6). But, like those same spices, if we do not learn how to manage our emotions, our lives become impossible to live.

Mickey Shea suffered from intemperance. Eddie's father, in his heroic leap into the sea to save the friend who had abused his trust, demonstrated temperance.

In these days, we think of temperance and intemperance primarily as a way of describing alcohol consumption, and it is certainly true that Mickey had a problem in that area. But that really doesn't describe the habit of temperance.

Temperance tells us how to bring the various parts of our lives into an ordered and unified whole. Just as justice is directed towards perfecting the relationships between persons, so temperance is directed towards perfecting the harmony within myself. The temperate man looks to himself and his own condition, seeking to bring it to perfection.

Though temperance is what orders a man, it is only realized, it is only expressed, in a man's relationship to other persons. In justice, a man is supposed to love God more than himself. In justice, he is to love others, who are the image of God, more than himself. A temperate man is the only man truly capable of justice. Only one who has rightly ordered the harmony within himself can rightly order his relationships with others.

> Mickey Shea suffered from intemperance.
> Eddie's father, in risking his life to his friend,
> demonstrated temperance.

Eddie's father jumped into the sea out of his sense of duty, but this was not just the duty he owed Mickey Shea. It was the duty he owed himself. By his leap into the sea and his own subsequent death, he showed that he was not blind to the relationship between

God and Mickey. He also showed that he honored that relationship; he acted to preserve it, even when Mickey did not.

He was able to show mercy to Mickey precisely because he loved himself enough, that is, he desired perfection enough, to image God. But there is even more here. He loved Mickey Shea enough to die for him precisely because He loved God and His perfection more than he loved either his own unperfected self or Mickey Shea.

Questions for Discussion

1. Why did Eddie meet Ruby and not Mickey Shea?

2. Given what has been studied so far, comment on the connections between courage and pain. Why is courage a consequence of other habits?

3. How would you explain to someone else that a man who willingly dies for a friend has just given a sterling example of a temperate, prudent life?

4. Why do so many people think hate is the opposite of love? Why is a good understanding of the doctrine of the Trinity absolutely crucial to seeing the error in that mode of thinking?

Scripture for Contemplation

Amos 2:6-7 – Crimes the Lord will punish.
Job 16:6 – The problem of pain.
Romans 8:17-26 – The reason for pain.

Further reading

The Four Cardinal Virtues by Josef Pieper
Heart of Virtue by Donald DeMarco

The Fourth Person:
Marguerite

Weddings

As Eddie prepares for his fourth meeting, he discovers his body is rapidly aging. It is literally rotting away. This raises an interesting question. Eddie clearly doesn't have a body in heaven – after all, death is the separation of soul and body and the novel clearly refers to his funeral. So what is going on here? Why does his heavenly "body" begin young and strong and slowly grow old and decayed?

There are two reasons, and they are related. First, as Eddie learns more about the life of virtue, his attachment to the world, slowly dies.

> For the whole law is fulfilled in one statement, namely, "You shall love your neighbor as yourself." … the flesh has desires against the Spirit, and the Spirit against the flesh; these are opposed to each other, so that you may not do what you want… Now the works of the flesh are obvious: immorality, impurity, licentiousness, idolatry, contraception, hatreds, rivalry, jealousy, outbursts of fury, acts of selfishness, dissensions, factions, occasions of envy, drinking bouts, orgies, and the like. I warn you, as I warned you before, that those who do such things will not inherit the kingdom of God.
>
> In contrast, the fruit of the Spirit is love, joy, peace, patience, kindness, generosity, faithfulness, gentleness, self-control.
>
> *-Galatians 5:14-23*

Eddie's actual body is in a coffin on earth. The body he sees in heaven is meant to represent the spiritual and psychological attachments he has to unjust ways of life, wrong habits of thought and action. We know that we are to become like a child in order to enter the kingdom of heaven, but we often misunderstand what this means. Children are capable of enormously clear sight about the world because they have few preconceptions. But children are also capable of enormous selfishness and self-centeredness (Matthew 11:16-19). We are to emulate the first set of qualities and reject the second.

Eddie's "body" began with the limberness of a child's because, while he had sufficient virtue to enter heaven, he was not yet fully perfected in virtue, he had not yet learned to deny himself, pick up his cross and follow Christ (Matthew 16:24). He clung to the ways of earth and had not yet fully learned any of the lessons of heaven. He is strongly attached to vices, he is limber enough to justify these vices to himself through whatever contortions might be necessary.

But, as he accepts each teaching in its turn, his "body" begins to bear the marks of the cross. At first it gains the strength of the soldier, ready for battle. He squares his shoulders, straightens his spine and prepares to face the facts. As he does so, his body slowly descends in power and beauty. He becomes aware of the weight of his own vice.

As noted above, the second reason is related to the first: "He was spurned and avoided by men, a man of suffering, accustomed to infirmity, One of those from whom men hide their faces, spurned, and we held him in no esteem" (Isaiah 53:3). As the others prepare him to stand before the beauty of God, his own glory fades.

"What is sown weak is raised powerful" (1 Corinthians 15:43). Many people are poor, but they gain no benefit from their poverty because they don't know how to use the strength of poverty. That is, they don't know how to use the life of virtue to prepare; they don't know how to consciously accept poverty in order to get ready for the inevitable. Rich or poor, wisdom is a rare virtue, and few know how to live it. As Eddie grows in his understanding of virtue, his "body" begins to live the poverty his spirit is learning to accept. But notice the difference between the control he has of his body and the control of the Blue Man, the Captain, Ruby or Marguerite.

Because each of them has fully accepted the life of virtue, they have gained complete control over their own bodies. At the end of their conversation, the Blue Man's skin becomes the most beautiful skin Eddie had ever seen. The Captain is no longer a smoker, Ruby can fly, Marguerite can change the apparent age of her body at will.

Eddie knows this growth in virtue is necessary at some level, but it is no small thing to walk away from an old set of habits and into a new. Transformation takes time, mostly because we need time to adjust to it and accept it.

> We know that we have passed from death to life
> because we love our brothers.
> Whoever does not love remains in death.
> *1 John 3:14*

So, though his attachment to wrong ways of thought and life begin young and strong, he is docile to the teachings he receives. His attachments grow older, weaker, they have less control over him. When they have no more power over him, he will gain complete freedom, as have those who gone before him.

Birth and Marriage, Life and Death

This is what promises are meant for, what sacrifices are meant for – persons. It is worth noting that the fourth person is the only one who has no baptismal symbol. As we have already seen, the meeting with the Blue Man was prefaced by immersion in the sea, the meeting with the Captain by pouring rain and the meeting with Ruby by ankle-deep snow. Even Tala, the fifth person, will be met on the banks of a river, but here there is no water. Why not? The answer is simple.

> Now a dispute arose between the disciples of John and a Jew about ceremonial washings. So they came to John and said to him, "Rabbi, the one who was with you across the Jordan, to whom you testified, here he is baptizing and everyone is coming to him."
>
> John answered and said, "No one can receive anything except what has been given him from heaven. You yourselves can testify that I said (that) I am not the Messiah, but that I was sent before him. The one who has the bride is the bridegroom; the best man, who stands and listens for him, rejoices greatly at the bridegroom's voice. So this joy of mine has been made complete. He must increase; I must decrease."
>
> *- John 3:25-30*

Baptism is intimately connected with marriage. It is, in fact, the beginning of the wedding feast. It is no coincidence that the jugs which held the water-turned-wine at the marriage in John 2 are called *baptismoi* in the Greek. John the Baptist names God the Bridegroom in the context of baptism. Thus, we can see that baptism is not only an entry into death, it is an entry into marriage.

Many a joke has been based in this fact. In this respect, the one who first spoke the joke and those who still smile at it are acknowledging an important fact: marriage is an enormous sacrifice. It is a death to one's self for the sake of the other.

Our lives have lost the meaning of marriage. Marriage is not simply about not being alone (the Blue Man), nor is it just about sacrifice (the Captain), it is about perfecting our ability to act justly to the other person, to order our lives in God's image, to courageously protect what is important (Ruby).

When we understand this, we can see that what we thought was simply baptismal imagery in the first three sections is also really marriage imagery. In fact, the two images are simply two sides of the same coin.

If we are to give ourselves totally to another person, we necessarily sacrifice our wants in order to fulfill another's. But here's the odd thing. In the self-gift I make to my spouse in marriage, I gain something I could never have otherwise gained. Like the shared meal, in which I sacrifice a portion of my food in order to feed another, in marriage I gain a level of communion with another person that would not be possible apart from the sacrifice marriage requires of me.

Men and Women

And it is in the context of marriage that more can be revealed. While Eddie's initial encounters in heaven were with men, his last three encounters were not. Ruby and Marguerite, his third and fourth persons, are women, his fifth person is the little girl. Again, there is a reason for that.

Many people have remarked on the great differences between the first two chapters of Matthew and Luke. Both tell of the events surrounding the conception and birth of the Christ child, but the similarities begin and end there.

> The life of a man can be understood only through the lens of a woman.

Matthew's account is filled with strange happenings and portents. Mary is mentioned barely four times and the birth of Christ is described almost in passing, quickly sketched in only half a verse. Instead, his narrative is devoted to the three kings, to Herod and his evil intentions, to Joseph's reaction to it all, how he leads his family to Egypt and leads them back home, and the divine guidance God constantly afforded him.

Luke mentions absolutely none of these things. Instead, Luke concentrates on babies: the events surrounding both Elizabeth's conception of John the Baptist and his birth, the events surrounding both Mary's conception of Jesus and His birth. We see how the families react to the events, we see Mary and Elizabeth talk together, we see how important the babies are.

Six major prayers of the Church and the very structure of the Mass come out of the first two chapters of Luke, no prayers or liturgy find their origin in Matthew. Why the difference?

Matthew is the infancy narrative told from a man's point of view. It tells men how to be fathers. Fathers stand between their families and the world, they stand on guard with their faces looking out. Whosoever tries to enter the family must first pass by the father. He protects the family from the world; he guides the family through the world.

Luke, on the other hand, tells the story of Jesus' infancy from a woman's perspective. Women maintain the communications within the family; they keep life intimate, closely connected, alive between all the members. Liturgy is the intimate union of Bride and Bridegroom. It is something that happens only within the family, only between spouses. It is the Wedding Feast, the Nuptial Feast, the consummation of all desire. Since Eucharist is the Body, Blood, Soul and Divinity of Jesus Christ, since it is the very Flesh of God, we can now see that it is at the Wedding Feast that the Flesh of the Bridegroom enters the flesh of the Bride, and we are imbued with life.

Once we see this, it is not at all surprising to find that, on his entry into heaven, Eddie meets men first. They teach him the virtues of poverty, sacrifice. They awaken him to the fact that he is not alone, he has never been alone. He learns the virtues of manhood from them.

But the women provide lessons in how to be a man that no man can offer, for they show him how to live the life of love. Ruby provides the bridge – the woman of the eternal banquet shows him what it means to live sacrificial love as a man. She does this by providing the window that shows him the sacrificial love his father lived. She is the doorway through which he finally begins to understand his father.

The life of a man can be understood only through the lens of a woman. It has often been remarked that Genesis has two creation accounts: chapter one and chapter two. Chapter one is an overview of the entire story of creation. Chapter two is a detailed description of the most important aspect of creation: the events of the sixth day, the creation of man and woman.

When we read Genesis 2, we must recognize that God wants us to gain a very deep understanding of how human persons are interdependent on one another. But more than that, He wants us to understand how much man and woman need each other. Man is not complete until woman is made. Creation is called "good" on every day, but it is called "very good" only at the end of the sixth day, after the creation of woman.

Woman is the last creature brought into existence. God saved the best for last in order to emphasize our relationship to Him: we are Bride to His Bridegroom, and it is because we are Bride that we are the best of Creation. Seen in this light, we suddenly realize that rejection of man's role as the crown of creation is really a rejection of woman's role as the better half of man.

Like Mary at the foot of the Cross, revealing her Son to all mankind, Ruby stands at the foot of the greatest pain in Eddie's life: his relationship with his father. Only after Eddie sees and accepts his father's life, shown through Ruby's lens, can he face the triumphs and tragedies of his own marriage. Now that he has seen how men are supposed to live sacrificial love, he is able to face how he lived, or failed to live, that same sacrificial life with his own wife.

To Have and to Have Not

His ability to sacrifice is most poignantly made clear in his last sentence. It is only when he openly states his attachment to Marguerite, "I never want to leave", that everything leaves him. Why? Because he cannot hold onto her and at the same time finish growing in the virtues.

"Do not touch me," said the risen Jesus to Mary in John's Gospel, "for I have not yet ascended to the Father" (John 20:17). This mysterious passage has long been discussed by those who study Scripture, but Eddie's life helps to illuminate it.

Mary Magdelene longed to hold Jesus as he was, the Jesus for whom she mourned, the Jesus who died on the Cross. She wanted things to return to the way they were. But they could not return to that state of affairs, she could never again hold the uncrucified Christ. Everything had changed. Christ was risen. She had to accept that change, grow, she had to become even more virtuous. Life could not be the same as it was prior to the Crucifixion. He did not go through the Passion - the suffering, the death – just to return to what had been.

> Eddie needs to be willing to let go even of *his* passion for Marguerite so that He might burn with God's passion for her.

"Do not hold onto me, but go to my brothers and tell them I am going to My Father and to your father, to My God and to your

God." She needed to embrace the new reality. Now it is fully revealed. Now is the time to prepare for the new life. It is the same with Marguerite. Precisely because Eddie expresses the desire to stay everything must change.

Ruby had already told him he could not return to Earth, but Eddie's desire is for exactly this – a return to the best moments of what he had on earth. Eddie grasps at the poorest of prizes, not realizing God intends for us even more than the best our life has to offer.

To enter heaven, we must not only surrender our pain, we must, in a certain sense, even surrender our joys. The greatest joy of Earth is as nothing compared to the least of heaven's joys. On Earth, Eddie loved Marguerite with a pure and passionate love. This enormous passion he held uniquely for her, but if he is to love Marguerite as she *should* be loved, he has to love even more. Like a man who releases a bundle in order to gain an even better grip, we must let go of what we have in order to grasp the enormous joy that is not yet in our reach. He needs to be willing to let go even of *his* passion for Marguerite so that He might burn with God's passion for her.

But this is poorly said. Let us speak in a different way and perhaps understand more deeply. Grace does not replace nature, it builds on nature. The natural love Eddie has for her will form the foundation of the perfect love God intends Eddie to have for her. He must let go now because his nature is not yet perfected. One step still remains. After that last step, God's grace can build on the perfected foundation.

The Gift of the Magi

Eddie and Marguerite were wed on Christmas Eve, when God's marriage to man is first announced to the world. In this way we know each spouse becomes a gift to the other, each is Christ for the other. But as Eddie and Marguerite know, our sins get in the way of our gift of self to spouse.

Now that Eddie has seen and accepted the level of sacrifice a man is called to, now that he sees his love again before him, he is so sorry he "can't say, can't say, can't say." In answer to Peter's three-fold denial and his bitter weeping over how he had betrayed his Lord, Christ healed him by providing an opportunity for the three-fold affirmation of love (John 22:15-17).

Peter denied Christ because he feared suffering. Eddie also fears suffering, he fears that his senses are betraying him, he fears that his love is not truly before him. In this sense, Eddie begins his encounter with Marguerite by denying the possibility that he has truly met his love. He then affirms his love for her by expressing his three-fold sorrow for all the things he had left undone for her. In her death, his loss and his new meeting of his love, Eddie experiences a taste of the death, the tomb and the resurrection.

It is at this moment that we can appreciate a wonderful attention to detail. "Marguerite" is French for "daisy." The daisy has long been a sign of the innocence of the Christ Child. Now we know why she bears this name. She is Christ to him.

> There is no fear in love, but perfect love casts out fear, for fear has to do with punishment, so one who fears is not yet perfect in love.
> *1 John 4:18*

Like the God who is the source of life, Marguerite begins the marriage with a desire to bear and treasure new life with and for her husband. She wants children. Eddie, whose soul is at war with itself, fears. He puts off children. He is too old. His father played cards, his son plays the horses. His father shattered the father-son relationship. Through sad circumstances outside his control, Eddie's chance to be a father likewise shatters.

With that shattering, Marguerite's faith and hope also shatter. Now she finds Eddie's fear creeping into her own soul. "There is no fear in love, but perfect love casts out fear, for fear has to do with punishment, so one who fears is not yet perfect in love" (1 John 4:18). Like Adam and Eve, who covered themselves to hide themselves from each other's gaze, so Eddie and Marguerite hide within themselves, afraid of being hurt. It is only on the edge of the sea that they find the fullness of their love again.

We all have loved someone who was taken from us before we were ready to let go. Whether it be mother, father, spouse, son, daughter, friend, it doesn't matter. Life is not complete. At least, it is not complete if we allow death to cut our love short.

Though love is not itself service, love leads to service, it is expressed in service. When the person who is loved is no longer there, we lose the ability to serve them directly. The joy of watching over and caring for another seems to be gone. But love is eternal. Every love is founded in Him Who is Love. We love because the person we love reflects some aspect of God.

God chooses each person to reflect something of Himself, and it is that reflection of divinity that each of us is meant to nurture and burnish in the other. No matter how deeply or how well we love a person, our personal encounter with God in heaven will create in us an overflow, a superabundance of love precisely because we will now recognize how much more perfect God is than His instrument. But even so, our love for the person who reflects Him will also grow, as we see even more clearly the likeness between that person and God.

No one goes unnoticed, no one can hide from His deep love. Our loneliness is self-imposed. We can live knowing that "we are surrounded by a great cloud of witnesses" (Hebrews 12:1) who surround us in love, or we can hide our eyes from the fact because we feel unworthy of it.

From the moment his soldiering brought him to kill, Eddie thought he had lost the ability to be forgiven. His sin was too heinous. He forgot the most important thing: God took flesh and died precisely to demonstrate to us that every sin can be forgiven. The only sin that cannot be forgiven is the sin we hide from God, the emptiness we refuse to allow His grace to fill.

Eddie speaks of God only twice, once to Ruby and again to Marguerite. The first time he asks in relationship to his father, the second time he asks in relationship to his sin. Through Ruby, he knows he can speak to His Father. With Marguerite, he contemplates what he must say to Him about their relationship, about his own sins.

Thus, though he spends endless weddings with his beloved, Eddie must return to the bride's preparation room. He has grown in the four cardinal virtues of prudence, justice, courage, and temperance. He has learned more about the theological virtues of faith, hope, and love. Now he must use all he has learned to prepare for the final cleansing.

When he tells Marguerite that he does not want to go on, when he says he wants to stay with her, he is really saying the same thing he told Ruby when he asked about returning to Earth. He knows in his heart what must come next, but he is afraid to face the hurt. His request that she appear as she did before her death is a recognition of this. The last time she looked like this, they separated. They must separate again. He knows it; he prepares for it, even though he does not want it. He is grown wise.

He knows in his heart the hurt must be healed. He knows Marguerite can do no more. He wishes it were otherwise. It is not. Like the first passage through the baptismal sea that is death's doorway, in the bride's room he loses everything except himself. But thanks to the four people who prepared him, he is now much closer to perfection. He is finally strong enough to be fully healed.

Heavenly Habits

Service

In marriage, each of us learn how to serve. Eddie recognizes Marguerite in her service to him. As she brings him chocolate almonds, she paraphrases her wedding vows, "for the bitter and the sweet" – for better or for worse.

We have lost contact with the meaning of marriage. Marguerite is Christ for Eddie. This is only proper. Marriage is the means by which we enter heaven; that is, marriage is the form through which divine grace reaches us. Let me explain.

God had called Adam and Eve to divine communion with Himself. Their refusal of His grace, their refusal to obey, is precisely what caused the great divorce between God and man. God healed the rift between God and man by becoming Bridegroom.

At the moment of the Incarnation, the Son married human nature to His own divine nature. That marriage of natures, accomplished in the womb of Mary - the virginal bride - is what began our salvation. His public ministry began with baptism, which John the Baptist identified as a wedding ceremony. He reserved His first miracle for a wedding feast, refusing to begin the work until the same virgin bride asked Him to accomplish it. His parables constantly refer to the wedding feast as the pre-eminent sign of God's kingdom. The last book of Scripture insists on describing Heaven as the Wedding Feast of the Lamb.

> Marriage is not about how my spouse serves me,
> it is about how I serve my spouse.

God saves us through marriage. Once we realize this, we can see that human marriage is a divinely appointed training ground. In this training ground, we practice how to love the Divine Person of the Son of God, our Divine Spouse, by living our love for a human person, an image of God. In a real sense, we serve our spouse as we serve Christ.

In the marvelous Italian movie, *Life is Beautiful*, the main character is training to be a waiter. In order to be a good waiter, he needs to know how to bow, but he does not do it very well. His uncle, the head waiter, gently corrects him, "Think of sunflowers. They bow to the sun. But if you see some that are too bowed down, that means they are dead. You are serving, you are not a servant. Serving is a supreme art. God is the First Servant. God serves man but He is not a servant to men."

Jesus models the life for us. We are to serve our spouse as Christ served the apostles and disciples. Christ serves us, but not as a slave. As a parent cares for a child, or a doctor cares for a sick man, so are spouses to care for one another. Proper service requires both full authority and fullness of love.

> Love is not an emotion.
> Love is a promise.
> It is the promise to serve another.

Thus, marriage is not about how my spouse serves me, it is about how I serve my spouse. The question every spouse must ask every day is not, "What has my spouse done for me lately? Is s/he helping me grow towards perfection?" These are entirely the wrong questions to ask.

Rather, we must each ask ourselves, "How have *I* served my spouse today? Have I helped him/her grow towards perfection?"

If I have not served my spouse, I am failing in my promise. I promised to serve for better or for worse, richer or poorer, in "the bitter and the sweet." The marriage vow is a vow to serve, to serve for life, to serve until death.

The One who is the Bridegroom hung on the Cross for the sake of the Bride. The best marriages are those in which both spouses race to the foot of the Cross. Whoever gets their first, whoever is willing to sacrifice self for the other's sake, wins. It is only there that "I live no longer I, but Christ lives in me" (Galatians 2:20).

Love

And here we see what faith and hope drive us towards: love. When the Blue Man had faith and hope restored, he realized the truth: we are never alone. Love is always present. Eddie had to learn about faith from the Blue Man, learn hope from the Captain, learn love from Ruby, and learn how all three fit together with Marguerite.

> We must live in our bodies
> what our minds believe.

St. Augustine saw that how we think and act take their cues from what we remember. In this way, our minds image God. The Father is Being, the Son is the Word, and the Spirit is the Love who pours Himself out upon the world. Eddie lives this sequence in the timeless time of heaven: he is first simply present (Being), then he begins to speak (Word), then he perfects his ability to love (Spirit).

Just as the Father's existence does not precede the existence of the Son or the Spirit, so Eddie's ability to be and speak does not precede his love: he has always loved Marguerite, but he learns what the fullness of Being, Word, and Love mean only in heaven with her.

It is only in the bridal room that Marguerite speaks of love. She knows it intimately. Love is not an emotion. It is a choice. As we know, the emotions of the body, what the body feels waxes and wanes. Emotions are, as Ebeneezer Scrooge pointed out, affected by a blot of mustard, a bit of beef broth. Scrooge made the mistake of assuming love was an emotion, a bodily function, a consequence of hormones. It is none of these things.

Love is a promise. It is the promise to serve another. Every day presents another opportunity to renew the promise, to make the sacrifice, to burnish the image of God we hold within us and to burnish the image of God we hold in our arms. We can love or we can flee. We can embrace each day's sacrifice or refuse it. There is no third choice.

With Marguerite's words, he finally understands that one of the sacrifices love requires is the willingness to allow the loved one to be perfected. We cannot reach perfection unless we give up everything for a time, even our bodies. If we truly desire perfect happiness for the one we love, then we must be willing to allow that loved one to endure the poverty - the training - necessary to reach perfection. Now, with Marguerite's disappearance, he finally knows what love is and what love demands.

But knowledge is not enough. We have seen how faith and hope are each a kind of knowledge. Love is also a kind of knowledge: "Adam knew Eve who conceived and brought forth Cain" (Genesis 4:1). With faith and hope, we see as through a dim mirror; with love, we see face to face.

But love differs from the other two in another way: love lives in action, it flourishes in service. Now that Eddie knows how to love, he must apply it. We are a sacramental people. That means that we must live in our bodies what our minds believe. Our bodies and our minds work together. This may seem trivial, but it is the secret to understanding every person you meet, the secret to understanding yourself. God desires all that we are, not just the spiritual soul, not just the body, but our total gift of self to Him, for He gives Himself entirely to us, and we are made in His image. We do what we see the Father do.

Questions for Discussion

1. How does the meeting with Marguerite complete his preparation for his final encounter?

2. Describe the differences between faith, hope and love. How is love related to service?

3. What did you learn about marriage that you had not fully realized before this?

4. Why is fear opposed to love?

Scriptures for Contemplation

Song of Songs 4:7- 5:1 – Bride imagery.
Ephesians 5:21-33 – Paul describes marriage.
2 Peter 1:3-4 – The goal of marriage.

Further reading

Sex and the Sacred City by Steve Kellmeyer
The Flesh of God by Steve Kellmeyer

The Fifth Person:
Tala

**Please read this section only after
you have completed Mr. Albom's book.**

The River

Eddie leaves the bride's preparation room and enters pure whiteness. He walks in white because he is now worthy (Revelations 3:14). His "body," that is, his attachments to old, bad habits of thought, is quickly decaying towards nothingness. He stands in silence, even as heaven stands in silence after the breaking of the last seal (Revelations 8:1).

Eddie has already closed his eyes; he has hidden his face as Elijah did upon hearing the still, small voice of God (1 Kings 9:12). Thus, Eddie is prepared to hear the still, small sound that echoes through the whiteness and gradually grows from intensity to intensity until he can recognize it.

He sees his fifth person standing on a white rock: "To the victor I will give the hidden manna; I shall also give a white stone upon which is inscribed a new name, which no man knows except him who receives it" (Revelation 2:17).

She calls herself "Tala." In Philippine mythology, Tala is the goddess of the stars. She has special connection to Venus, the morning star: "I will give him the morning star" (Revelations 2:28, 22:18). Thus, his fifth person is a girl whose name connects her both to Jesus and to "the woman clothed with the sun, and the moon under her feet and on her head a crown of twelve stars" (Revelation 12:1).

Tala begins by teaching him a new language. She asks him for a gift. Only after she has received the gift, a hound of heaven, does she tell him the last secret.

He is the one responsible for her death. He killed an innocent. Her very purity makes him aware of the depth, the consequences, of his actions, both good and bad. Now that he is prepared to handle it, now that he has been strengthened and renewed in his understanding, only now does he experience the soul-wrenching agony of knowing what his own sins have done to the world. Only now does he enter into the fullness of purification.

It is in this moment, in the moment when he washes the very ground with his tears and the Spirit Himself intercedes with inexpressible groanings that he begins to see himself in proper relationship to God (Psalm 6:6, Romans 8:26). His cry becomes like unto the loud cry of Christ on the Cross as the last shreds of his own life are torn from him (Mark 15:37). Christ cried out for mercy upon the poor sinners who crucified him, Eddie cries out for mercy as one of the poor sinners who has held and hammered home the nails.

The river is, of course, the most powerful symbol of baptism in the book. "And he showed me a river of water of life, clear as crystal, proceeding from the throne of God and of the Lamb" (Revelation 22:1). It is here, in the river of heaven that Eddie is able to make reparation for what he has done. Tala, the innocent he killed, asks him to wash her in the river.

> Then he went down and washed in the Jordan seven times… and his flesh was restored like the flesh of a little child, and he was made clean.
> *2 Kings 5:14*

Though he cleanses her, it is himself who is being cleansed; the consequences of his sin are stripped from her skin by the stone she hands him. Just as Mary gave to Christ the body that Christ used to conquer sin, so Tala gives to Eddie the stone that he uses to strip the consequences of his own sin from her body. She rests in his arms as he washes her. Only after the cleansing does he become aware that this washing is also completion: she is the fifth and last person.

"Then he went down and washed in the Jordan seven times… and his flesh was restored like the flesh of a little child, and he was made clean" (2 Kings 5:14).

Our Purpose-Driven Lives

We each have a purpose on this earth, a specific goal to accomplish in order to assist Christ's work of healing the world. If it is no more I who live, but Christ who lives in me, then what I do must mirror what Christ does. Christ's work is the salvation of the world, I am part of the Body of Christ, so my work is also the salvation of the world. Jesus does not need me to accomplish this work – He can do it by Himself. But He desires me to participate. I am to "make up what is lacking in the suffering of Christ, for the sake of His Body, the Church." (Colossians 1:24).

Eddie fears that he failed. His continuous, endless sorrow on earth derived from the fear that he was not accomplishing the task that had been set before him from the beginning of the world. Because he had spent his whole life in loss and sorrow, because he had failed to live to its fullness the life of virtue God had ordained for him, he had always felt useless, like Sysiphus bent under his boulder.

Tala points out the truth. Man is not called to win. Man is called to serve. We serve him in our sorrow as well as in our joy, in our failures as well as in our successes. We may spend our whole life in what appears to be failure and loss, but what we see is not necessarily the reality of what is. Our sorrow, our failure, our loss may lay the necessary foundation for ultimate triumph. "For the foolishness of God is wiser than men, and the weakness of God is stronger than men… if I must needs glory, I will glory in the things that concern my weakness" (1 Corinthians 1:25, 2 Corinthians 11:30).

> This is why no life is a loss, nor is suffering ever without meaning or dignity.

Eddie did what he was meant to do. He maintained the rides and thereby saved the lives of thousands of children. Because he lived the life of virtue as best he could under the dominion of weakness and sin, God supplied the lack and completed the work. This is why no life is a loss, nor is suffering ever without meaning or dignity.

Now, with the acceptance of this truth and the surrender of all barriers, his purgation is almost complete. His purification lacks but a single thing: a single question remains unanswered. "Am I like my father? Am I like the Father? Have I saved a life?"

He knows that he took the life of an innocent girl, but did he save the life of an innocent girl? His father leapt into the ocean to save his friend, his enemy. Eddy leapt into the jaws of death to save a little girl he did not even know. Did he imitate his father? "Amen, amen, I say to you, he that believes in me shall do not only the works I do, but greater works besides" (John 14:12). Did he live, no; did he *die* as he was called to die? Is he worthy of his Father's love?

> "Did I save her? Did I pull her out of the way?"
> Tala shook her head. "No pull."
> Eddie shivered. His head dropped So there it was. The
> end of his story.

In his last question to Tala, she allows him to live the understanding: even his last burning question must be surrendered to the will of God, to the perfection of God's plan. At the last moment, even his one small hope of personal triumph is allowed to die so that it, like Christ, might be resurrected and given its proper meaning and proper glory.

> "Push," Tala said.
> He looked up. "Push?"
> "Push her legs. No pull. You push. Big thing fall. You
> keep her safe."

In that death and resurrection, he discovers triumph, not just his own personal triumph but a greater. He discovers the triumph of his Father's love.

> "But I felt her hands," he said. "It's the only thing I remember. I *couldn't* have pushed her. I felt her *hands*."

> Tala smiled and scooped up river water, then placed her small wet fingers in Eddie's adult grip. He knew right away they had been there before.

> "Not *her* hands," she said. "*My* hands. I bring you to heaven. Keep you safe."

That which my Father hath given me is greater than all: and no one can snatch them out of His hand.
John 10:29

She, the innocent who was slain by his hands, is the one who takes him by the hand, leads him to heaven, keeps him safe. These five people have taught him how to do in heaven what he tried to do through the virtues he lived on earth. With this last, full purification, with this last death and resurrection in love, with this last touch of baptismal water, he has given all that he is to God. Now he understands love. Now God begins to glorify him.

He submerges into the water and his "body," all his attachments to his old way of life, all the consequences of his sins, everything is washed away. He feels beneath and around him the stones that made up the stories of his life: "Come to him, a living stone, rejected by men but chosen and made honorable by God. Be like living stones; let yourselves be built up into a spiritual house, a holy priesthood, to offer up spiritual sacrifices acceptable to God by Christ Jesus" (1 Peter 2:4-5).

Tala holds him, guides him through this loss of the old and birth of the new. She guides him through the river that cleanses us of all pain and suffering (Revelations 22:1-2). He ascends through the waves of the great sea and becomes fully aware of how his life changed the lives of others. The sea now gives up its dead, and he rises to new life (Revelations 20:13).

Now he is ready to pass on what he knows: all the individual stories of mankind are one story and each of us are part of it – the story of Christ in the world.

> For this corruptible must put on incorruption:
> and this mortal must put on immortality.
> And when this mortal hath put on immortality,
> then shall come to pass the saying that is written:
> Death is swallowed up in victory.
>
> O death, where is thy victory?
> O death, where is thy sting?
>
> *1 Corinthians 15:53-55*

Questions for Discussion

1. Eddie killed many people in the war. Why did Eddie meet the little girl instead of someone else, the Japanese soldiers who held him captive, for example?

2. Purgatory is often called "the mud-room to heaven," because it is that part of heaven where we are made perfect before we meet God. Discuss how this concept applies to this story.

3. Discuss the strong Marian aspects of this book. How is this another example of "all generations shall call me blessed"?

4. Has this study given you an urge to learn more about the virtues? What will you do in the coming weeks to prepare more fully for the inevitable?

Scriptures for Contemplation

Revelation 22:1-7 – Description of the river of life.
1 Corinthians 3:10-15 – Description of purification.
Matthew 18:1-5 – The greatest in heaven's kingdom.

Further reading

The Many Faces of Virtue by Donald Demarco
Bible Basics by Steve Kellmeyer

Afterword

A habit is an acquired mode of behaviour that is relatively involuntary: it is something we do without thinking. "Virtue," says Augustine, "is a good habit that is in harmony with our human nature."

How can something good be in harmony with human nature? This can only be true if human nature carries some remnant of goodness. Virtue can exist only if human nature is not totally corrupted.

God made every human person in His own image and likeness. These two terms are used without anyone bothering to define what they mean. Yet, if we do not understand what this phrase "image and likeness" means, we cannot grow in virtue.

God is Three Persons: Father, Son and Spirit. When we speak of man being made in His image, we mean that we are persons. Our personhood is a consequence of, a gift from, God Himself. We know many things about the Trinity, but this we know more firmly than anything else: since there is but one God, the Three Persons of the Trinity can never be separated. We can distinguish between the Persons, but we cannot separate the one divine substance from itself.

The Three Persons are distinguishable only by their relationships: Father begets Son, Son is begotten by Father. Father and Son together breathe forth the Spirit, the Spirit is breathed forth by the Father and the Son. These relationships of begetting and begotten, breathing and being breathed – are crucial. If it were not for relationship, the Three Persons within the one Godhead would not exist.

If relationship is that important to the Persons of the one God, then it is certainly going to be that important to us human persons. Indeed, because we know this about God, we know something about ourselves: we are persons only because God has called us into relationship with Himself. If He had not done this, we would be human animals: human beings with a full human nature, but without a personal relationship to God. It is not our nature that makes us persons; rather, it is God's call to each of us that makes us persons. Since He desires a personal relationship with us, since He empowers us to be in this relationship with Him, we are each persons.

This is what it means to say that we are made in God's image. It means we are called into a relationship of intimate communion with God. It means we are persons.

But what of likeness? We are like God in the sense that we share in His power. His power is pre-eminently the power to be in communion with Him. Grace is power. In a word, grace is "likeness."

So, to be in God's image is to be the subject of His call. To be in His likeness is to be given the grace, the power, to answer that call.

Adam and Eve were made in the image and likeness of God. They were called into intimate personal communion with God and they were given the power to live that communion. They rejected the power. As a result, their likeness to God was deeply wounded. In rejecting grace, they lost so much of their power to commune with God that they had not the power to restore the communion.

However, God's call to them, God's call to us, does not change. That is, they kept God's image. They remained persons, just as we are still persons. They just didn't have the power to live out what it means to be fully human persons. We are fully human only when we are doing what we are made to do: live in communion with God.

But, despite Adam and Eve's error, God's grace springs new every morning (Lamentations 3:23). Every day, He sends us the grace we need to restore us to Himself. Our good habits – our virtues – are our response to that grace. If we use His grace to train ourselves in living the four cardinal virtues: prudence, justice, courage and temperance, then we can learn to respond to even greater gifts of grace: the theological virtues of faith, hope and love.

All the good habits, all the virtues of our life are directed towards just one virtue: love. Indeed, each virtue, even the virtues of faith and hope, are really just aspects of love. By studying the individual aspects of how to love, by practicing those individual habits in our daily lives, we learn what love is. We learn how to make our life resonate with it.

> For this is good and acceptable in the sight of God our Saviour, who will have all men to be saved and to come to knowledge of the truth.
> *1 Timothy 2:3-4*

But habits are not easy to change. This is both good and bad. If we have a good habit, a habit in accord with right reason, then a new circumstance or the suddenly increased weight of an old circumstance will elicit from us the same good response. Unfortunately, if we do not have a good habit, we are likely to respond badly when these same circumstances demand a response.

Like a runner training for a prize, we must train our minds and our bodies to habitually turn towards God and away from sin. That is what St. Paul describes in 1 Corinthians 9:24-27. He tells us what Eddie also learned – training is hard, painful work, but it is necessary if we are to become fully human. And that is what heaven is about: making us fully pure, fully in communion with God, fully human.

In the end, *The Five People You Meet in Heaven* is a story built around a simple fact: "There shall not enter into heaven anything defiled or that works abomination or that makes a lie" (Revelation 21:27). It is my hope that this work helps each of us respond to God's grace and build our lives towards that goal.

About the Author

Steve Kellmeyer has a master's degree in theology from Franciscan University, Steubenville, Ohio and a master's degree in history from Southern Illinois University, Edwardsville. He is a popular speaker and writer who specializes in adult formation, Catholic apologetics, and JohnPaul II's Theology of the Body.

He has written over one hundred articles for various Catholic newspapers, magazines, and websites and currently writes regularly for the Catholic Radio Association newsletter, *The Radioactive Messenger*. A popular speaker who skillfully shows how theology applies to today's headlines, he appears frequently in lecture halls and on radio stations across the nation.

Other books by Steve Kellmeyer include:
Bible Basics
Sex and the Sacred City: Meditations on the Theology of the Body
Fact and Fiction in The Da Vinci Code
Artfully Teaching the Faith
The Flesh of God

Please see the following pages for a short description of a few of these offerings.

Artfully Teaching the Faith

Did you know that many of the greatest medieval and Renaissance artworks were specifically intended to teach Catholic doctrines?

This short book introduces you to twelve masterpieces of Catholic history, and matches each to a doctrine of the Church. By studying the commentary along with the on-line art images, you will learn how to decipher the symbols embedded within each piece of art.

- Discover how Michelangelo depicted the three Persons of the Trinity and the dual natures of Christ by studying his Creation of Adam!
- Learn to read the symbols in the most famous Christian icon ever created!
- Discover why a masterpiece depicting Mary resting with the infant Christ on the way into Egypt is actually a foreshadowing of the Last Supper!
- Find out why a nineteenth century artist put a crumpled rug in his vision of the Annunciation.

You will quickly gain an appreciation and an appetite for discovering the Faith in the most beautiful way possible, using beauty itself!

Masterpieces include:

Creation of Adam - Michelangelo
Incarnation - Fra Angelico
Matthew Inspired by an Angel - Guido Reni
The Last Judgement -Michelangelo
Vierges Aux Anges - Bouguereau
Icon of the Blessed Trinity - Rublev
The Transfiguration - Raphael
Christ Giving Peter the Keys - Perugino
Disputation on the Eucharist - Raphael
The Baptism of Christ - David
The Wedding Feast at Cana - David
The Rest on the Flight into Egypt - David
The Incarnation - Henry Ossawa Tanner

You have the questions.
Bridegroom Press has the answers.

www.bridegroompress.com

We have the resources you need.

Sex and the Sacred City
Meditations on the Theology of the Body

Already being used in high school vocation classes and for engaged couple marriage prep, marriage retreats, and adult individual and small group study, this is a book any busy person can immediately use:

> "First of all, I wanted to say thanks for the preview of "Sex and the Sacred City." I liked it so much that we're making it one of the textbooks for our Vocations class next year. What a concise, powerful reflection on Theology of the Body."
> **-Kevin Kiefer**, Blessed Trinity Catholic High School

> "In just a hundred pages Steve Kellmeyer distills the rich and complex Theology of the Body. *Sex and the Sacred City* is a masterpiece of clarity. It's size, stylistic grace as well as it's logic should guarantee this book wide readership. Rarely is such a dense topic so delightfully explained and for adults as well as adolescents at that!"
> **- Al Kresta**, President-CEO of Ave Maria Radio

Each of the nine chapters has a study guide with questions, Scripture and Catechism references to help the reader get a basic understanding of Pope John Paul II's Theology of the Body. Come read this celebration of sexuality and discover why John Paul II has spent his entire pontificate explaining the vital role sexuality plays in our discussion of both God and ourselves!

www.bridegroompress.com

We have the resources you need.